It's Been

A

Long Time

Coming

Poetry by Leroy Meadows

Copyright © 2017
Leroy Meadows

First Printing
Bethune Publishing House, Inc. The Bethune Group
All rights reserved, including the right
to reproduce this work in any form whatsoever
without written permission from the publisher,
except for brief passages in connection with a review.
Photographs may not be reproduced without
permission of the owner.

For information write:
Bethune Publishing House, Inc.
P. O. Box 2008
Daytona Beach, FL 32115-2008
admin@tbginc.org Phone: 386-999-0092

Cover designed by John-Mark McLeod
J2maginations, LLC J2maginations@gmail.com
Book design and page layout by
Bethune Publishing, Inc.

Printed in the United States of America
Library of Congress Control Number:
2017945583
ISBN: 978-1-946566-03-4

It's Been

A

Long Time

Coming

TABLE OF CONTENTS

TITLE	PG #	TITLE	PG #
The Beginning	4	Opportunity	44
For People	5	Dear Jane	45
You Are You	6	Ghetto	46
Law	7	Passion	47
We Exist	8	Outcome #Two	48
You Poem	9	Count to Ten	49
Union	10	One Dime	50
Moving Mountains	11	Best Behavior	51
Everybody	12	To Lillie	52
Persevere	14	Answer to Your Questions	53
And So On And So Forth	15	Life	54
To Whom It May Concern	17	For Now	55
Sequence	19	You Deserve It!	56
Bowaa	20		
Outcome #One	21		
Now	22		
Nobody	23		
A Fifteen Word Poem	24		
To A Libra Brother	25		
To Leo (Happy Father's Day)	28		
The Student	29		
Wisdom	30		
Repeat	31		
Saturday Noon	32		
Finish	33		
God Damned	34		
Age	35		
The Crap Game	36		
The Lyrics	39		
The Operas	40		
Grateful	42		
If I Could Cry	43		

The Beginning

Every day starts
As a blank canvas.

For People

Death is definite.
Living is painful.
Laughter – a response
And tears flow from feelings.
Hate is a protection.
Love is a gift.
And no one loves
A confused man.

To touch is an urge.
Being hurt – a necessity.
Doing is an act
And waiting is a task.
Sympathy is given
And respect is earned.
And no one respects
A confused man.

Life is a game.
Work – a word.
Distance is from here to there
And time is a measurement.
A song is music
A scream is a loud cry.
And a confused man's scream
Is never heard.

You Are You

Isn't it wonderful…
    You are you.
Only you can be you.

Wherever you go
    You are there.
Whatever you do
    You do it.

If you are tall
    You are tall
If you are short
    You are short.

You are unique.
You are the only you
    There will ever be.

Law

The one thing
Always holding a person down
Is gravity

We Exist

We exist on planes.

We are now between
the
before-life
and the
after-life.

We can travel
to the before
and
recall the
experience
in this plane.

We can travel
      to the after
      and realize the inevitableness
      in this plane.
On three plane… We exist.

You Poem

If this poem could
      brighten the world
The way your smile
      lights up the day

If a word could
      mean as much as
      the sound of your voice

If a rhyme could be all things
      wonderful and sweet

It would be you.

Union

The heart has a say
      In every decision
      The mind makes.

Moving Mountains

The way to move
a mountain
is a handful at a time
And though some may
      slip through
      the fingers
it can be picked up and moved again.

The way to move
a mountain
is a stone at a time
A rock is lifted
A boulder is rolled away.

The way to move
a mountain
is bit by bit.

Everybody

Bob wants Alice.
Alice wants Fred.
Fred wants Bob.
Any of them will tell you
 If you don't want
What they want
What you do want
Ain't good for you.

The Russians drink vodka.
The French drink wine.
The Mexicans drink tequila.
Any of them will tell you
If you don't drink
What they drink
What you do drink
Ain't good for you.

Truck drivers take No-Doz.
Housewives take Ny-tol.
Junkies shoot up.
Any of them will tell you
If you don't do
What they do

What you do do
Ain't good for you.

Everybody wants to do
Their own thing
And wants to bother
Everybody else
About their thing
Because their thing
Ain't the same thing
As their thing.

Persevere

All hardships
      are tempered
      with
Innumerable blessings.

And So On And So Forth

They were alone.

A voice was singing softly
    on the stero.
The night was beautiful.

Their lips met
    in a gentle kiss
and they moved slowly.

The musical interlude
    had
violins playing.

The moon was full
    and they held together tightly.

There was the sweet scent
    of flowers entering through the open
window.

They were in love.
Then, there was silence.

The moonlight gave bright tones

to their skin colors.

And another song started almost unnoticed.

    They moved slowly.
    It was late.
The song built to a symphony
    and choir finale.

    Then, the sound of a baby
    singing could be heard
    in the future.

    And so on and so forth.

To Whom It May Concern

This letter is not
Addressed to everyone,
But to the people that it refers.

You have just one life.
There is no such thing as
Reincarnation, heaven or hell.
Just death.
So live your life to its fullest.

Try to do as many things as
You feel you want to
Or have to do.

Laugh when you want
Any place or any time
You feel you want to
Or have to.

Sing when you want to,
Talk whenever you feel like talking.

If you feel like running
Run while you can.

Sleep all you like

And eat all you like.

It's your life –
Do with it as you please.

This might not apply to you,
And it might not apply to me,
But it does apply
To those whom it may concern.

Sequence

The answer
      presents itself
      before
The question
      presents itself.

Bowaa

A baby with small
    soft hands.
An old watch, rusty
    from time
These are Bowaa.

A lone light showing
    brightly.
Neon lights gleaming
    on a city street.
These are Bowaa.

Seeing nothing but
    nature for miles.
Watching the passing
    people in buses and cars.
These are Bowaa.

The rising of the sun
    in the morning.
A cool evening breeze,
    These are Bowaa.

Bowaa.
Beautiful.
You.
You are Bowaa.

Outcome #One

I've made some good choices
For some bad reasons.

Now

Every new moment is
A new moment.

Nobody

Nobody wants
Like they need
And
Nobody really
Really Cares

You're just a lonely boy
Standing all alone
Thinking you have no one
No one you can call your own.
And this world
This world
It cries for you

"Where is she? Where has she gone?"
She should be back inside
Inside your heart
Her home

See?
She's standing all alone
Feeling oh so blue
Thinking she's no one
Nobody wants
Like they need
And
Nobody really
Really
Cares.

A Fifteen Word Poem

If I said there are
      fifteen words in this poem
Would you bother
      to count them?

To A Libra Brother

You tipping way over
      my man
      your eyeballs rolling
      way back in your head.
      Ghosts?

Hun...
The fat miller knows what it is.
      Ghosts?

Yeah.
White on your mind
      ripping off your manhood
      ripping off your courage
      ripping off your strength
      ripping off your will
      ripping off your brain
      ripping off
You're in a nod now?
      Forgot about the girl
      they found with the peace(sic)
      still in her arm?
      Forgot about the guy
      shot over a piece

cut eighty times?

Yeah.
You have hooked up with something
    badder than you
    deadlier than you
    you're shooting
    a bad boy.
Can't you see what it is now
    (with your eyeballs
    rolled way back
    in your head?)

Down.
Down.
Down.
Down.

That's where it's taking you
    who your little brother
    was going to look up to.
    Who was 'Mister State'.
    Who hides in the bathroom now
    to cook?

Yeah you.
Kicked in the arm

by a white thing that's tearing
your body down.
Ghosts?
Hun...
The fat miller knows what it is.

To Leo (Happy Father's Day)

Dear brother
Life has brought
Ups and downs
But your strength and encouragement
Has always helped us in overcoming
Another day.
Your laughter, your wisdom,
Your insight into daily trials
Has helped form healthy outlooks
As we grew from kids to adults.
I am sure the charity and goodness
And love
You shared as a boy
Is continually given as a man,
A father.

The Student

Every six weeks
He brought home
All A's
And she sat
On the sofa
Impregnated
By his nine-year-old
Pee stains
And dreamed dreams
Of his future.

Wisdom

When you read
More than you think
You will know
More than you think.

Repeat

You are human.

Young, but there is strength in your youth.
You are growing into a world that will
Get larger and larger than the little
Place where you came from.
But you must continue to open your eyes
To see all that is behind you
And beyond you.
You must care for your body
And keep it strong.
You will have some enemies
That seem like friends-
You must be able to see
The difference.
It may seem hard
But that is the way it is.
Life is easy for you.

You are human.
Always remember.

Saturday Noon

His smile became so bright
So white
That it burned flaming red
And became all of him
And his arms were upstretched
Above his head
And he was the devil
And all the children
Screamed, hollered
And ran out of
The theater!

Finish

When you run out of things to do do something else.

God Damned

God. Damned.
God or damned?
Either this or that –
God or damned
and that's a fact.

Like up or down.
Left or right.
God or damned
that's the fight.

God or damned –
That's the choice.
Everybody has a voice.

God or damned
that's not a curse,
there is good
and there is worse.

God. Damned.
Truth versus confusion.
God the real, damn the illusion.

God Damned.

Age

One knows
      one is getting old
When one has
      a different story
      to tell
      to better explain
      anything better
      than one can.

The Crap Game

What?????!
Somebody giving away money tonight??!

I say he don't make five –
Who wanna bet two?

Chump, you don't wanna bet nothing
If two's the best you can do!

Move aside –
Let me through!

Come on hot mommas
You know what I want you to do.

Five say he seven out.
Five say you'll shut your mouth.

Look out fellas –
Here they come!

Five!

I just love to take your cash.

Put up or shut up the trash!

Come on heaven –
Gimme some seven.

You'd be surprised

At what your money buys.

Snake eyes !!
All them lies!

Roll 'em somebody!
I'm hot!

Ten say he don't nine.

Well that's just fine.

Here's ten more
If you wanna take mine.

Come on dice –
You know what to do.

I'm with him –
Anybody betting two?

Let's see 'em roll man.
Don't be praying all over the dice.

Jesus – Nine !
Don't they look nice?

I like to take your money.
You pay off real slick.

I got a bad feeling
I'm gonna get sick.

Seven. Seven.
Gimme a four and a three

You gonna bet man,
Or are you standing round here
For free?

The Lyrics

Happiness,
 love,
kindness,
friendship.
Hum the melody.

The Operas

They are tux and tails
jeans and flannels,
Cowboy boots,
Silk, satin, velvet, lace
And sometimes
nothing.

They are in the white house
the jail house
the play house
the bar
the church

They are soothing, stimulating,
provocative
pulsating

They are hot and heady
soft and throbbing
wild
and controlled

They take the usual
the obvious
the unsuspected turns

They appeal to the
high and low
sick and strong
rich and poor

Wherever there is a set.
They are now
They are today
Except
Saturdays and Sundays.

Grateful

I am thankful
my last breath
was not
my last breath.

If I Could Cry

If I could cry I would
Have tears in my eyes
When I think about
The hard times my parents had.

If I could cry I would
Weep every time I am
Beat by clubs and rifle butts.

If I could cry my eyes would
Be clouded each time
I am debased and
Treated like an animal.

If I could cry my head would
Be bowed when others
See my insecure state.

If I could cry, I would be crying now.
But I have overcome.
I cannot cry.

Opportunity

In every moment
There is a choice.

Dear Jane

You left me.
The joy in my
     life is gone.

You left me.
My short-lived happiness
     has ended.

You left me.
Now I wonder
     'What can I do?'

You left me
and there's one thing
     I can't deny:

I miss you.

Ghetto

The first time
I remember littering
I was told to take the garbage out
And the trash can was full
So, I threw the busted bag
In the alley
With other bags

Like it?

Passion

I strive to
      be better
to
      be better
to
      be better
to
      be better…

Outcome #Two

I've made some bad choices
For some good reasons.

Count to Ten

They say if I count
    to ten
        I'll feel better.

One. Two. Three.

By the time I get
    to ten
        I won't be angry.

Four. Five. Six.

By the time I get
    to ten
        I won't be mad.

Seven.

    I won't be violent.

Eight.

    I won't be destructive.

Nine.
I feel better.

One Dime

I have just one dime.
Should I use it to try to call friend
    in hopes of getting more
    money?
Should I hold it for fifty years
    then trade it in
    as a rare coin?
Should I use it to buy
    a cake or a fruit?
Should I throw it over my shoulder
    for good luck?
I had just one dime.

Best Behavior

Mind
And remind
Yourself.

To Lilly

My love for you is like the love
      That has been song about
      In all the love songs.

It is like the strong love
      That has been told about
      In stories since the beginning
      Of time.

It is like the softness of a kitten,
      And the urge in a man
      Dying of thirst yet still
      Trying to get water.

But it has its own special quality
      Because it is
My love for you.

Answer to Your Questions

Me?
I'm me
What I got to
Have to
Want to be.
See?

Me?
Laughed a lot.
Thought life was
Fun and games.

Told a lie or two
     Three
     Four
     Five
     Six
     Seven…
Yeah.
I'm me.

Life

The mind is the parent.
The body is the child.

For Now

Woman
Don't weep for me now.
      Comfort me.
If I fall, help me up
    and I'll continue
      to fight for
Don't weep for me now

When I'm gone
When I'm gone.
Maybe.
A tear.

You Deserve It!

Thank you.
    Thank you.
Yes, thank you.
      Thank you.
Thank you, thank you.
      And, thank you.

www.ingramcontent.com/pod-product-compliance
Lightning Source LLC
Chambersburg PA
CBHW050508120526
44588CB00044B/1796